To

From

To Mr Mills and Brookfield Primary School K.W.

Text by Lois Rock
Illustrations copyright © 2013 Kay Widdowson
This edition copyright © 2013 Lion Hudson

The right of Kay Widdowson to be identified as
the illustrator of this work has been asserted by
her in accordance with the Copyright, Designs
and Patents Act 1988.

Published by Lion Children's books
www.lionhudson.com
Part of the SPCK Group
SPCK, Studio 101, The Record Hall, 16–16A Baldwin's
Gardens, London EC1N 7RJ

ISBN 978 0 7459 6383 9

First edition 2013

Acknowledgments

Bible extracts are taken or adapted from the
Good News Bible published by the Bible Societies
and HarperCollins Publishers, © American Bible
Society 1994, used with permission.

The Lord's Prayer (on page 81) as it appears in
*Common Worship: Services and Prayers for the Church
of England* (Church House Publishing, 2000) is
copyright © The English Language Liturgical
Consultation and is reproduced by permission of
the publisher.

A catalogue record for this book is available
from the British Library

Printed and bound in China, May 2024, LH54

tiny tots
Bible

Retold by Lois Rock
Illustrated by Kay Widdowson

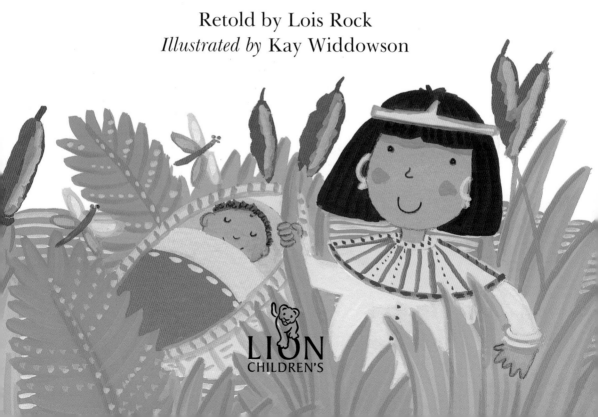

LION
CHILDREN'S

Contents

In the beginning   6

Noah and the ark   10

Abraham and the promise   16

Joseph and the dream come true   22

Moses and the long way home   28

Joshua leads the way   34

David and Goliath   40

A little girl and a big river   46

Jonah and the deep, dark sea   52

Daniel and the lions   58

The baby born in Bethlehem   64

The wise men and their gifts   70

How to be good   76

Jesus and the storm   82

The little girl   88

Loaves and fishes   94

The man who stopped to help   100

The lost sheep   106

Here comes the king!   112

The first Easter   118

In the beginning

Before there was anything
there was nothing.
Deep, dark nothing.
And God.

sparkle

God spoke. "Let there be light."

twinkle

6

God made everything under the sun:
amazing things, astonishing things,
and everything just right.

shine

God made people.

"Your name is Adam," said God to the man.

To the woman God said, "Your name is Eve."

"This world is your paradise home. It will give you all you need.

"Take good care of it."

Noah and the ark

Noah sighed. He could hear arguing. Again.

"I want to end all this badness," said a voice. Noah gasped. *It was God's voice.*

"I'm going to send a flood," said God.

"Noah, build a great big ark for you, and your family, and a mother and a father of every living thing."

So Noah did.

The rain came.
  The flood rose.
  In all the world there was only Noah
and the ark
and God.
  The bad old world was gone.

13

At long last the rain stopped.

The flood trickled away.

"It's time to begin the world all over again," announced Noah.

A rainbow spread across the sky.

"I promise," said God, "never to send a flood like that again. There will be summer and winter, sowing time and harvest time for ever."

Abraham and the promise

Abraham was sitting outside his tent and feeling sad.

"I have made my home in this land," he said. "I have sheep and goats and cattle.

"But I have no son who can live here after me."

God spoke.

"Look at all the stars!" said God. "One day there will be as many people in your family. They will my people, and they will show the world what I am like."

Abraham smiled. "I shall put my trust in God," he said.

17

But the waiting went on and on.

Abraham's wife Sarah watched the children playing.

"They are all other people's children," she said to herself. "Abraham is so sure that one day I will have a son.

"But can I still believe that, after so many years waiting?"

19

Then it all came true.

Abraham and Sarah did have a son. They were very happy!

They named him Isaac, and the name means "laughter".

"Now it is easy to believe," they agreed. "God has blessed us, and through our family God will bless everyone."

Joseph and the dream come true

Joseph loved showing off in his new coat. "My father gave this to me," he said, "because I'm the son he likes best.

"More than that, I dreamed that one day all my family will bow down to me."

His ten older brothers scowled.
"Not if we can help it," they agreed.
When they got the chance, they sold him
as a slave.

In faraway Egypt, Joseph was a nobody.

But God was looking after Joseph and made him wise.

When the king had troubling dreams, only Joseph could say what they meant.

"You must store food when the harvest is good," said Joseph, "to last when the harvest is bad."

"Good idea," said the king. "Joseph, you're in charge of that."

When the harvests did fail, Joseph's brothers came begging to buy food.

They didn't recognize Joseph as they bowed down before him.

At last, Joseph understood. His dream was coming true… but for a good reason.

"God has taken care of me so that I can take care of you now," he said.

He forgave all his brothers. He welcomed his family to Egypt.

Moses and the long way home

Slowly and carefully, the mother was making a basket.

"It's a cradle to keep your baby brother safe," she told Miriam.

"The cruel king of Egypt wants our boy babies thrown in the river. We won't let his soldiers find your little brother.

"We'll hide him in the river."

Together they hid the baby and the cradle in the reeds.

Miriam watched as the princess found him.

"I love him," said the princess. "But who will care for my little Moses?"

"I'll find someone," cried Miriam. She brought her mother.

When Moses grew up, he felt sorry for his people because the bad king was mean to them and made them work as slaves.

But he got into trouble for trying to help them and had to run away.

One day in the wild country, God spoke to him from a bush that seemed to be on fire.

"I am choosing you to lead my people out of Egypt," said God.

"Take them to the land that is to be their home."

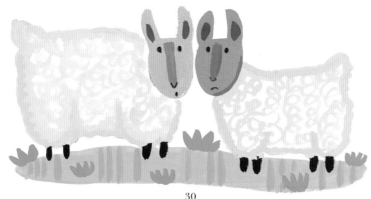

The king of Egypt didn't care about the God of Moses. He did not want to let his slaves go free.

"If you go against God," warned Moses, "there will be trouble."

And so it was. In the end, the king let the people go.

God made a way through the sea so that they could escape.

Now they were free to live as God's people should, and to show the world God's love.

Joshua leads the way

When Joshua was young, he was a little bit scared of Moses.

"He is the leader," he told the other boys, "and he speaks for God.

"The laws he tells us to obey are God's laws. They are written on stone to show they must last for ever."

When Joshua was a young man he became a soldier. He was hardly ever scared of anything.

"It's not enough to be brave," he told the other soldiers. "When we fight, we are fighting for God's laws, so we must obey them."

When Moses grew old, he made Joshua the leader. Joshua led the people into the land that would be their new home. The walls of Jericho barred the way.

"Fetch the golden box in which we keep the law stones," he said. "We will march with it around the walls."

For six days they marched and blew their trumpets. On the seventh they marched, blew their trumpets, and then shouted very loudly.

The walls fell down. Joshua and the people took the city.

When at last they had made all the land their home, Joshua called the people to a meeting.

"I promise always to obey God's laws," he said, "the laws about love and kindness. Will you obey these laws?"

"Yes we will!" everyone cried.

David and Goliath

David was a shepherd boy.

Sometimes, when he was watching the sheep, he sang songs to God and played his harp.

Sometimes he threw stones with his sling.
"To scare off hungry animals, like YOU,
Mr Wolf."

One day, he took a basket of food from home to his brothers. They were soldiers, fighting the people's enemies.

A giant came out of the enemy camp.

"I am Goliath! Who dares fight me?" he roared. "Beat me and you win the war."

"I dare fight him," said David. "I dare because I trust in God."

He slung a stone that hit Goliath.

The giant fell down. David had won!

For years David was a fighter. He beat all the people's enemies. Then he became king in the city of Jerusalem.

Sometimes he liked just to sing songs to God and play his harp.

The Lord is my shepherd
and I am his sheep:
he finds me green pastures
and ponds clear and deep.

The Lord is my shepherd:
though danger be near
my Lord will defend me –
I've nothing to fear.

A little girl and a big river

The little servant girl smiled as she did her work.

"You are brave and good," said her mistress, "and very forgiving.

"I know you were captured when my people fought your people."

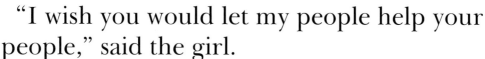

"I wish you would let my people help your people," said the girl.

"Your husband, Captain Naaman, has a horrid skin disease.

"Among my people is a wise man who could cure him. He has power and wisdom from God."

Captain Naaman set off with rich gifts.
  The wise man, whose name was Elisha,
heard about his arrival. He sent a servant
to him with a message.

"Go to the River Jordan and wash in it seven times."

Naaman was angry. "We've got nicer rivers in my own land," he cried. "Why should I do that?"

"Please," said his own servants. "Just try."

Naaman went and washed in the River Jordan just as Elisha had said.

He was completely cured! More than that, Elisha did not want any gifts.

Naaman went home a changed man.

"From now on," he said, "I am going to say my prayers to the God who made me well."

Jonah and the deep, dark sea

God had told Jonah to go to Nineveh with a message.

Jonah was angry.

He did not like what God had said.

"I will not go to Nineveh. I will not give them God's message.

"The people there are wicked. They are the enemies of my people."

Instead, he hurried down to the sea and got on a boat.

"I shall go as far away as I can," said Jonah.

The boat set sail. In the night, a storm blew up.

"Some great god wants us to die," wailed the sailors.

"No," said Jonah. "The greatest God of all wants me to deliver a message.

"Throw me into the sea and the storm will stop."

The sailors threw Jonah into the deep, dark sea.

God sent an enormous fish to swallow him whole.

The fish swam to a beach and spat Jonah out.

"I know what to do," said Jonah.

He hurried to Nineveh.

"Listen to the greatest God of all," he told them. "Change your wicked ways or there'll be trouble."

The people of Nineveh were sorry for being wicked.

They changed their ways. And God forgave them.

Daniel and the lions

Daniel did not live in his homeland. His people had been beaten in war. They had been taken as captives far away.

Daniel still remembered his homeland. He still said prayers to his God.

Other men frowned.

"We don't like Daniel," they agreed, "because the king gave him the best job.

"Let's tell the king that he's not loyal.

"Let's say that Daniel thinks his God is more important than the king."

They asked the king to make a new law: anyone who thought anyone was more important than the king should be thrown to the lions.

Then they went and found Daniel at prayer.

"He's broken the law!" they told the king.

The king was very upset. But his new law was the law.

In the lions' den, God kept Daniel safe.
The king was delighted.
  "Bring him out," he ordered. "Now
everyone needs to know this: Daniel's God
is the One and Only."

The baby born in Bethlehem

Mary gasped when she saw the angel.

"Don't be afraid," said the angel Gabriel. "God has chosen you to be the mother of a very special baby.

"You will name him Jesus. He will save people from all that is wrong and bad.

"He will help them do what is right and good.

"He will bring God's blessing to everyone."

Joseph was startled when he heard the angel's voice.

"Marry Mary," said the angel. "Take care of her and the baby she will have."

Not long after, they had to travel from Nazareth to Bethlehem.

All the proper rooms were full.

"I have a stable that is quite cosy," someone offered.

And that is where Mary's baby was born.

Out on the hillside, angels appeared to some shepherds.

The shepherds were amazed when they saw them.

"Good news," said an angel. "Tonight, in Bethlehem, a special baby has been born. He has come from God in heaven to bless the world."

The shepherds went and found Joseph and Mary and little baby Jesus.

Then they knew that everything the angels had said was for real.

The wise men and their gifts

The night sky was glittering with stars.

"The new star shines more brightly," said the stargazers.

"It is a sign that a new king has been born."

They set off to find him.

70

71

They came to
Jerusalem and asked
about the king.
　"I'm king," said
King Herod angrily.
　"We know," agreed
everyone in the
palace. "But in our
very old books are
very old promises:
that one day God will
send a special king.
He will be born in
Bethlehem."
　"Ah," said King Herod. "I'll send the
stargazers there."

The star shone on the road to Bethlehem.

It led the stargazers to the place where
Jesus was with his mother.
   They gave him rich gifts:
gold, frankincense, and myrrh.
   Gifts for a king.

How to be good

Jesus grew up in Nazareth.

At school he learned to read God's laws from the treasured scrolls.

At home he learned to do the same job as Joseph.

Then, when he was grown up, he set off to do the work that God had sent him to do: to tell people how to live as God's friends.

Crowds gathered to listen.

"Do for others what you want them to do for you," Jesus said. "That is the meaning of God's laws.

"Love everyone – the people who are kind and the people who are unkind.

"Always forgive them.

"Then God will forgive you. God will take care of you."

"When you pray, say this:

"*Our Father in heaven,*
hallowed be your name,
your kingdom come,
your will be done,
on earth as in heaven.
Give us today our daily bread.
Forgive us our sins
as we forgive those who sin against us.
Lead us not into temptation
but deliver us from evil.

"Remember this: your Father in heaven wants to give good things to those who ask him."

Jesus and the storm

Jesus chose twelve people to be his friends and help him in his work.

Some of them were fishermen, sailing their boats on Lake Galilee.

Now they used a boat so that Jesus could travel to lots of towns and villages on the lake shore.

After one very busy day preaching, Jesus got on the boat and fell asleep.

His friends sailed the boat.

In the night a storm blew up. The wind roared. The waves crashed.

Even the fishermen were scared.

"Help!" they cried. "We're going to sink!

"Wake up, Jesus, wake up."

Jesus stood up.
  "Hush," he said to the wind.
  "Lie down," he said to the waves.
  At once the lake was calm.

"Oh my," whispered the friends. "How can Jesus do that? He really is someone very special."

The little girl

The little girl's father had one hope left. Everyone said that Jesus could make sick people well. He needed to believe that.

And Jesus had just arrived in town by boat.

"Please Jesus," he begged, "please come and make my little girl well."

"Of course I will," replied Jesus.

But there was a big problem. Crowds of people wanted to see Jesus, wanted to touch Jesus. And Jesus was stopping to talk!

A messenger arrived for the father.
"Jesus doesn't need to come now," he said.
"I'm sorry. Your little girl has died."
The father burst into tears.
"Don't worry," said Jesus. "Only believe."

He went to the house.

He went to where the little girl lay still on her bed.

"Little girl," said Jesus, "get up."

And she did. The mother and the father laughed for joy.

Loaves and fishes

Whenever Jesus spoke, he told people about God's love.

The crowds wanted to listen to everything he said. One day, a huge crowd stayed for hours and hours.

Jesus spoke to his friends.
"We need to give them something to eat."
"We have nothing to give!" they cried.

"We have got something," said the friend named Andrew. "This kind boy wants to share his food: five loaves and two fish."

"That's good," said Jesus. "Tell everyone to sit down and get ready to eat."

He took the food and said a "thank you" prayer.

"Now give some to everyone," Jesus told his friends.

By a miracle, there was enough for everyone.

"And all these leftovers!" said the friends. "Twelve baskets full!"

The man who stopped to help

What really pleases God? Jesus told a story to help people understand.

"There was once a man who went on a journey. Out on the lonely road, robbers came and beat him up. They stole all he had and left him lying in the road.

"A priest from God's Temple in Jerusalem came along. He saw the man in the road, but then he hurried on by.

   "A helper from God's Temple came along. He walked over to look at the man. Then he hurried on by.

"The next person who came along the road was from another part of the country. He never even went to God's Temple.

"Even so, he stopped to help. He bandaged the man and took him to an inn.

"What do you think?" asked Jesus. "Which of the three men did what pleases God?"

The answer was easy: the one who was kind.

"And," said Jesus, "you should do the same."

The lost sheep

Jesus often said that God loves people and wants to be friends with them.

Not everyone liked that. "Look at his followers!" they said. "Some live very bad lives. "Can anyone believe God wants them as friends?"

Jesus told them a story.

107

"A shepherd had a hundred sheep.
  "One went missing.
  "So what did the shepherd do?
  "He left the ninety-nine and went to look
for his lost sheep.

"When he found it, he was overjoyed.
  "God is like that shepherd.
  "God wants to welcome those who have lost their way."

Here comes the king!

It was festival time. Lots of people were going to the Temple in Jerusalem to say thank you to God for his love and care.

"Here comes Jesus," cried someone.

"Hooray," cried the crowd.

"Hooray for God's chosen king."

The people in charge of the festival at the Temple were very angry.

"Wherever you go, you upset things," they told Jesus. "Stop it, or there'll be trouble."

Jesus was sad. "Look out for those people," he told his friends. "All they care about is themselves. They say long prayers but they don't care about people in need."

When it was time for the festival supper,
Jesus and his friends were together.
Jesus shared out the bread.
He shared out the wine.

"I won't always be with you," he said.
"You must meet to share a meal like this,
and remember me."

The first Easter

The people who did not like Jesus made a wicked plan.

They captured Jesus one dark night when no one dared to help him.

They told lies about him.

They had him put to death on a cross.

Jesus' friends laid his body in a tomb. They rolled the stone door shut just as the sun was setting. It was time for the day of rest.

The day after that, as the sun was rising, some of them went to say a last goodbye.

The tomb was open. Angels spoke to them. "Jesus is not here. He is alive!"

Soon they saw Jesus for themselves.
  Then they knew:
  God's love can never be beaten.
  God's love and forgiveness are for everyone.
  "Now go and tell everyone!" said Jesus.

125

And with God's help, they did!